My Father Was a Toltec

Poems by Ana Castillo

My Father Was a Toltec

Poems by Ana Castillo

West End Press
1988

Some of these poems have appeared in the following publications: *River Styx, Canto al Pueblo, Revista Chicano-Riqueña, Fem, Haight-Ashbury Literary Journal*, and *Poetry San Francisco*.

This book was kicked into shape by Las East 28th Street Girls c/s: Norma "la Heavy" Alarcón, Cherríe "La Puente" Moraga, Yvonne "La Fregona" Yarbro-Bejarno—"¡Carnales a todo dar!"

Heartfelt thanks also to my editors John Crawford and Pat Smith, and to Tony Herrera for his computer assistance and moral support.

First edition—September, 1988
ISBN 0-931122-49-x

Back cover photograph © 1987 by B. Böhner
Design by Patt Gateley
Typography by Prototype

This project is partially supported by a grant from the California Arts Council, through funding provided by the National Endowment for the Arts, a Federal Agency.

For more copies, send cover price times number of copies prepaid to: West End Press, Box 2510, Novato, CA 94948.

TABLE OF CONTENTS

IN MY COUNTRY

For the daughters of Latino men everywhere
y en memoria de mi querida doña Jovita

I
The Toltec

THE TOLTEC

c. 1955

My father was a Toltec.
Everyone knows he was *bad*.
Kicked the Irish-boys-from-Bridgeport's
ass. Once went down to South Chicago
to stick someone
got chased to the hood *
running through the gangway **
swish of blade in his back
the emblemmed jacket split in half.

Next morning, Mami
threw it away.

*neighborhood
** in Chicago, the space between buildings that leads to the alley

ELECTRA CURRENTS

Llegué a tu mundo
sin invitación,
sin esperanza
me nombraste por
una canción.

Te fuiste
a emborrachar.

RED WAGONS

c. 1958

In grammar school primers
the red wagon
was for children
pulled along
past lawns on a sunny day.
Father drove into
the driveway. "Look,
Father, look!"
Silly Sally pulled Tim
on the red wagon.

Out of school,
the red wagon carried
kerosene cans
to heat the flat.
Father pulled it to the gas
station
when he was home
and if there was money.

If not, children went to bed
in silly coats
silly socks; in the morning
were already dressed
for school.

SATURDAYS

c. 1968

Because she worked all week
away from home, gone from 5 to 5,
Saturdays she did the laundry,
pulled the wringer machine
to the kitchen sink, and hung
the clothes out on the line.
At night, we took it down and ironed.
Mine were his handkerchiefs and
boxer shorts. She did his work
pants (never worn on the street)
and shirts, pressed the collars
and cuffs, just so—
as he bathed,
donned the tailor-made silk suit
bought on her credit, had her
adjust the tie.

"How do I look?"
"Bien," went on ironing.
That's why he married her, a Mexican
woman, like his mother, not like
they were in Chicago, not like
the one he was going out to meet.

THE SUEDE COAT

c. 1967

Although
Mother would never allow
a girl of fourteen to wear
the things you brought
from where you wouldn't say—
the narrow skirts with high slits
glimpsed the thigh—
they fit your daughter of delicate
hips.
And she wore them on the sly.

To whom did the suede coat with
fur collar belong?
The women in my family
have always been polite
or too ashamed to ask.
You never told, of course,
what we of course knew.

DIRTY MEXICAN

"Dirty Mexican, dirty, dirty Mexican!"
And i said: "i'll kick your ass, Dago bitch!"
tall for my race, strutted right past
the black projects,
leather jacket, something sharp
in my pocket
to Pompeii School.
Get those Dago girls with their teased-up hair
and Cadillacs,
Mafia-bought clothes,
sucking on summer Italian lemonades.
Boys with Sicilian curls got high
at Sheridan Park, mutilated a prostitute one night.
i scrawled in chalk all over sidewalks
MEXICAN POWER CON/SAFOS *
crashed their dances,
get them broads, corner 'em in the bathroom,
in the hallway, and their loudmouthed mamas
calling from the windows: "Roxanne!" "Antoinette!"
And when my height wouldn't do
my mouth called their bluff:
"That's right, honey, I'm Mexican!
Watchu gonna do about it?" Since they didn't
want their hair or lipstick mussed they
shrugged their shoulders 'til distance gave way:
"Dirty Mexican, dirty Mexican bitch."
Made me book** right back, right up their faces,
"Watchu say?" And it started all over again . . .

* in Chicago, "If you don't like it, come to me"
** go

FOR RAY

i found a stash of records
at the Old Town Street Fair.
Gave up Perez Prado,
"Rey del Mambo,"
to Ray.

But Cal Tjader's
Soul Sauce
Guacha Guaro
cooler than
a summer's night breeze—
Della Reese in spaghetti strap
dress cha-cha-cha—
is *mine.*

And who am I?
A kid on the güiro
who no one saw jamming
scrawny and scabby kneed
didn't sing Cucurucucu Paloma
or Cielito Lindo but happy
to mambo
please to teach ya
all of seven then . . .

Now, with timbales
and calloused hands
not from a career of
one night stands but the grave
yard shift on a drill press,
Ray thrills the children
who slide in party shoes
at Grandpa's house where
the music blares and it's
all right guacha guaro
guacha guaro it's all right.
My daddy's still *cool.*

DADDY WITH CHESTERFIELDS IN A ROLLED UP SLEEVE

The school principal was a white lady
who came to class one day
to say a man claiming to be
my father
was in her office.

Later at Tío Manuel's flat
Daddy said Mami was
on her way. (*It must be serious,*
i thought, Mami never misses work.)

All Manuel's tribe gathered:
rotten toothed daughters with children
of varying
hair textures and surnames;
David, a junkie,
mean face of an Apache;
Daniel, smiled nice, did nothing
with his life;
Abel and his boy Cain;
Juanita my madrina, the eldest,
never married.
Twelve children my uncle raised,
his wife died with the 13th.

But this guy across the table
is young with acne,
hair greased back. He smokes cigarettes,
doesn't ask permission, speaks English
with a crooked smile: charm personified.
Hangs out with the boys,
who call him Brodock (they all have
names: Ash Can, Monskis, El Conde,
Joe the Boss, Ming)—this man, who Mami says
doesn't like to work,
plays bongos and mambos loud all day
while Abuelita keeps me out the way
of boys jamming, drinking beer,
while wives work the assembly line.

At Tío Manuel's where Daddy took me on the bus,
the Spanish radio has announced
the death of Doña Jovita.
The curandera from Guanajuato—
with jars of herbs
grown in coffee cans—
had raised the Toltec long
after her sons had grown,
her only daughter murdered by her husband.
The boy, the story goes,
was brought forth by the curandera,
or, if you please,
Doña Jovita, herself,
gave birth to him at 60.

And Daddy, who never looks at me
and talks to me at the same time
says "Granny died," and begins to cry.
Daddy is the only one
who calls her Granny.

And i, most delicate of her offspring:
Ana María. Ana María learns English in school,
wears gold loop earrings in mother-pierced ears,
brings flowers to the Virgin every spring.

Anita knows yerba buena, yerba santa, epazote,
manzanilla, ruda, addresses spirits
with Abuelita, touches soreness of those
who come, little hands under
shriveled ones, that heal.

"Granny died," he said, and cried.

Daddy's white foreman
who doesn't believe his mother died,
comes to watch Daddy cry at the coffin.

Every year Mami makes enchiladas for Daddy's birthday,
never as good as the memory of his mother's.
Mami takes her place now,

tells his daughter to her face:
"You're like your father,
don't like to work,
a daydreamer,
think someday you'll be rich and famous,
an artist, who wastes her time
travelling,
wearing finery she can't afford,
neglecting her children and her home!"
The father lowers his eyes.

"Granny died," he said, and cried.

Had i been 19 not 9
i'd have pulled my hair,
screamed her name, "Don't leave!
Don't leave me behind with this mami
who goes off to work before light
leaves me a key, a quarter for lunch,
crackers for breakfast on my pillow
that rats get before i wake!
Don't leave me
with this mami who will empty out all
your jars, the trunks of your defunct
husband's moth-eaten suits,
the Toltec's wind-up toys,
to move bunkbeds into your
room where you stuck crucifixes
with chewing gum on an old iron headboard!
(A testimony to your faith—
yet the Church did not grant you a Mass
upon your death.)
Don't leave me with this daddy,
smooth talkin', marijuana smokin',
mambo dancin', jumpin' jitterbug!"

The only woman who meant anything in his life.

—No creo que fue tu mamá, —your wife whispers.
"I don't care!" you reply.

12

—Que ni eres mexicano, —
"I don't care!" you say for
Doña Jovita,
la madre sagrada
su comal y molcajete,
la revolución de Benito Juarez y Pancho Villa,
Guanajuato, paper cuts, onyx, papier-mâché,
bullfighters' pictures, and Aztec calendars.

i speak English with a crooked smile,
say "man," smoke cigarettes,
drink tequila, grab your eyes that dart
from me to tell you of my
trips to Mexico,
i play down the elegant fingers,
hair that falls over an eye,
the silk dress accentuating breasts—
and fit the street jargon to my full lips,
try to catch those evasive eyes,
tell you of jive artists
where we heard hot salsa
at a local dive.
And so, i exist . . .

"Granny died," and you cried.

At 15,
Mami scorned me for not forgiving you
when she caught you
with your girlfriend. Had i been 25,
i'd have slapped you, walked out the door,
searched for Doña Jovita who loved for no reason
than that we were her children.

Men try to catch my eye. i talk to them
of politics, religion, the ghosts i've seen,
the king of timbales, Mexico and Chicago.
And they go away.
But women stay. Women like stories.
They like thin arms around their shoulders,

the smell of perfumed hair,
a flamboyant scarf around the neck
the reassuring voice that confirms their
cynicism about politics, religion and the glorious
history that slaughtered thousands of slaves.

Because of the seductive aroma of molé
in my kitchen, and the mysterious preparation
of herbs, women tolerate *my* cigarette
and cognac breath, unmade bed,
and my inability to keep a budget—
in exchange for a promise,
an exotic trip,
a tango lesson,
an anecdote of the gypsy who stole
me away in Madrid.

Oh Daddy, with the Chesterfields
rolled up in a sleeve,
you got a woman for a son.

II
La Heredera*

*The Heiress

ALTERNATIVES

yes—yes
we—no
so
maybe i can be
an " exotic" version
of Pati Smith / strike
lewd poses for Fan-Belt
Mag / make heavy comments to
Time like " i'm into Razor Blades,
mon, double edged, of *coarse* " / my shaved
head back up could call itself Los Razor
Blaids and wear shark skinned suits without
collars and very pointed high heeled boots / my
poems would emit musk—and would NEVER be repeated
excepted by electronic sound and to make it that much
more heavy, mon, i'd muffle the mike with pantyhose so
nobody would know how heavy i really was and up would go
the acoustic guitar to accent the poetry of my ever so heavy
mammary glands and that's how they'd remember me in Paris before
I toured Morocco and sent Japanese adolescents en masse to Spanish
courses in Tokyo figuring i was too heavy to be reciting in Yankee tongue
and Beirut loved me because i wasn't exotic but actually a long lost Lebanese
compatriot and X-mas holidays i'd relax in the Caribbean or Mexico, right off the
coast, of course, where not even the tourists would recognize me, so naturally brown
Indian brown, before the tan and my working class folks back in Chicago would still be
wondering when I was going to settle down to a decent, stable job although the postcards
are nice and the cover picture on *People* was something to save for the relatives in San
Antonio but so blurred it was hard to tell it was really me next to those pelones that
travel with me and are becoming unworthy millionaires off my brains and possible talent
and all this happened shortly before i was taken to a hospital with my wrists intact
since I wasn't really into razor blades but something sawed through a very delicate
place in my head and it split in two precise halves so that i was assigned a very
bland room without doorknobs on the inside and without bars but the windows did
n't open anyway and my mother knew it all along when it was discovered that my
manager ran off and spent all my investments but being the hard but silent
type she said nothing the day i came " home " talking about teaching or going back to the University of Chicago for a PhD but what would i live
off of meanwhile and i remember my long ago ex-husband who would be
married to a truly exotic, non-English speaking girl who went into
labor when she found i was back and hadn't even needed a visa and
it would be October because autumn is when bones turn yellow and
all things return to what they once were or really never stopped
being.

FOR NO ONE, OR PERHAPS YOU

i am carnival
annual holiday from
work and tedium
your masquerade
as mythical hero: marbled
Ulysses. i am Sundays
at the matinee
a fifty cent piece
for candy and popcorn
your first party where girls
formed a motif on the opposite
wall, the last dance of your youth
as dawn broke and you went home alone;
the taut seconds before she
turned the corner,
whose mouth was freshly baked bread,
both your faces flushed
with virginity.

i am the one
with whom you play Houdini.

i am Rome
Rio
Paris
the villages of Mexico
the house maids therein,
that certain actress whose
celluloid thighs were magnified
in their perfection.

i am the spy
in the hole of your conscience.

WOMAN OF MARRAKECH

As if i were Fatima
you have sex with me
and go away,
Fatima who dances
for men, without one
of her own
who has no inheritance
no home, nothing. Fatima,
whose brother comes after her
with a knife. She is shame.
As if i were sex personified
you remember the way to my
city, my street, the house
where you don't dare knock.

Sex is seven hundred hotel
rooms in Paris, one of them
ours and unused.

It has been a month, one
menstrual cycle. i am a
fly stuck to the light, an
hysterical speck on a linen
collar. You have so many
important things to do. i am
Fatima
a woman
sex.

RECORDANDO UN DISPARATE

Llamaste. Se me olvidó cuanto antes que
te havia olvidado.
Llegaste después. Desde luego me quitó
el disgusto. Como niños jugamos.
Me traías un regalo hecho por tus manos:
—se llama "Disparate."— Sonreí de acuerdo.

Quise besarte y te besé. Era una tarde
(ayer, para ser precisa) cuando el calor
era aún tolerable.

Querías saber por que no andaba por la playa,
tomando aire y sol en vez de estar vestida
de gitana, escuchando discos y pensando
en poemas nuevos. Y tú tan pálido
se que tampoco te asoleas . . .

Y cuando iba a tocar otro disco tú
salias del baño peinado y oliendo
a mi jabón.
—Me voy, Madame—dijiste.
—Si, como es tu costumbre—dije yo.
—Y antes me crucificas, como es la tuya—
contestaste.
—Siempre traes tus propios clavos y tu cruz.—

Te fuiste. El beno que me quisiste dar
se esfumó en el aire. Me fui a bañar
cuanto antes, tenía un compromiso a las ocho.

AN UGLY BLACK DOG NAMED GOYA

An ugly black dog named Goya
witnessed through
glass doors
a woman's legs high
on its master's shoulders.
Goya's tongue hung
panting loud.
Her eyes challenged
Goya's, she called out:
—¡Mira ese perro cochino!—
Thrust interrupted,
irate master threw a shoe,
dog ducked, dejected
by a slew of insults.

From a corner
locked in shadows
Goya pretended to sleep.
Early grey winter inhaled
late afternoon,
obscuring this one—
nothing like his mistress
who was pale and thin,
nervous as a bitch,
brought him fresh meat,
said gaily: "Here, Goya, baby!"
and who was afraid
of men
passing joints on the street,
waiting for tenants
to leave
so they could enter
back windows,
the mistress who cried
one night: "You can have
this dump! I'm going back
to Forest Hills!"

She always phones
at dusk just
to see if another woman
is there
but by then,
the master alone
at work with paints,
canvas, color, books,
and Wagner,
has stopped yelling
at the dog named Goya
too grotesque with hybridism
not to be mean,
lets him lie
near his feet
until the heaviness of winter
exhales a semblance
of light
and they both get to sleep.

ENCUENTROS

encuentros
sobre
consomé de pollo
café de olla
cuando
dos países
dos puntos de vista
dos mundos distintos
se enfrentan
cara a cara

            él a ella
            ella evita pregunta
            tras pregunta

empiezan
a quejarse
de tortillas frías
mendigos que paran
a comer con sus ojos
sin vergüenza
mientras

            el sol desparace
            sigue siendo día

"dicen
que en francia
no se bañan"
ella habla
fusilando
un ambiente sin
chiste

            "parece
            que va a llover"
            viene
            la respuesta

Y aún no se les
ocurre preguntar
sus nombres

MI COMADRE ME ACONSEJA

Mi comadre me aconseja que te olvide
pero siempre he sido una mujer
que a fuerza deja fermentar sus recuerdos,
como las 30 años de inviernos,
la mayoría fueron
más impenetrables que la verga del diablo,
como la madre que me dio
su último beso el día de mi primera comunión,
que fue también
cuando su marido la dejó.

—Tu padre, tu padre,
ese hombre, esos hombres,
que no trabajan
que no les importan a sus hijos
que no más andan con la bebida
y tras de las faldas,
esos hombres—

Y nadie, ni mi comadre sabe
cuanto me gustas

aún más, cuando te hago sufrir.

LA HEREDERA

Soy
de huesos finos
de cabello liso
que se convierte
en hilos dorados
en el verano
soy toda de oro.

En un dedo
el anillo
cuyo brillo atrae
tu mirada
a mi mano,
el cigarillo
a los labios llenos
que forman un beso,
el encendimiento
invita a los ojos
negros
que se cierran
como barreras.

LAMENTO DE COATLICUE

Cierro los ojos
y estás aquí
convertido en noche
Tezcatlipoca,
hijo malcriado.

Después vienen
los cadáveres
a rodearme, y aún
no he abierto
los ojos.

Recuerdos quebradizos
de huesos amarillos.

TODO ME RECUERDA TU AUSENCIA

Colgando la ropa
sobre un mecate afuera
de la ventana
la neblina me recuerda Madrid,
y tu ausencia. Todo
me recuerda tu
ausencia.

En ese piso en Madrid,
se abrian las ventanas así,
como ésta. Todas las vecinas
se empinaban colgando
toallas, sábanas y calcetines.

En la calle, en el frío
de enero, las manos de las damas
se arrugaban como "papier-mâché"
mientras fumaban sus cigarillos
y lucían sus pieles de zorro.

Me seguías entonces, como ahora
me sigues por los museos, como
por mi cocina, cuando pongo a
cocer los frijoles, y le sirvo
la leche al niño.

Es por demás.
Tus capacidades de araña me
encuentran en cualquier lugar.
Si me cuelgo yo misma de
un mecate afuera de la ventana,
estoy segura, me seguirás.

POEM 13

i too
can say
good-bye
effortlessly
silently
remove
myself
from an undesired
space
turn about face
march forward
never
look over
my shoulder
control
memory
erase unnecessary
experience
deromanticize
romance
wind tomorrow
around me
without company
(freeze my womb)
publicize my birth
given name

i too
can be my
mother's child
become my father's
extension
improved upon
gesticulate courage
profess pride
am worth
that much
i too
could live satisfied
with all my acts
content
amidst my ignorance.

FOR JEAN RHYS

1890–1979

Well, hell, shit
sometimes it gets
pretty damn difficult
trying to understand
the human race, don't it?
Exercising language
the species' claim to fame,
instead of just humping
the first being that
goes by.

He talked throughout the night
gave 300 pages
of his unwritten memoir:
the stint
in military school,
narrow escape
from the Jesuits,
the uncle sent to Siberia,
and the present wife,
whom he first loved
in dreams.

She hardly edged in a word
like the last body in the metro
before the train goes off.
She smoked his cigarettes and
drank the bordeaux,
all the while, not losing sight
(in that practical manner
he so obviously detests)
that she was only there
due to circumstances.

At last, calculated sighs, even tears
punctuated with a "Well?"
to heighten the drama.
"Well what?" she replies.

"Well, will you have sex
with me or not?"

Well,
she could have gone to a park
sought asylum in a police station:
"I've been robbed."
100 report forms, the sun up
she'd go out to mix with the crowd.

All she needs is sleep,
in a safe place.
In the morning she'll go out
to mix with the
ruddy faced workers
of nicotine stained teeth
who ride the metro
with a gaze of irradicable
detachment.

She steps out of the bathroom,
powdered cheeks gone limp
like wet clay and leaves,
hardly angry.
Anger was affordable at age 25.
Disillusion long ago an expense.
Now, she has only to find
a place to sleep.

And this morning,
pink dawn above Paris, magenta
where city smog fuses with sky,
she has a cafe crème on the street
and goes on. No one will notice her
once she mixes with the crowd.
A bag for a pillow,
a coat to keep her warm,
the loud screech of rails,
a subterranean lullaby.

III
Ixtacihuatl Died in Vain

IXTACIHUATL DIED IN VAIN*

I

Hard are the women of my family,
hard on the mothers who've died on us
and the daughters born to us,
hard on all except sacred husbands
and the blessings of sons.
We are Ixtacihuatls,
sleeping, snowcapped volcanoes
buried alive in myths
princesses with the name of a warrior
on our lips.

II

You, my impossible bride,
at the wedding where our mothers
were not invited,
our fathers, the fourteen
stations of the cross—

You, who are not my bride,
have loved too vast, too wide.
Yet I dare to steal you
from your mother's house.

It is you
I share my son with
to whom I offer up
his palpitating heart
so that you may breathe,
and replenish yourself,
you alone, whom I forgive.

III

Life is long enough
to carry all things
to their necessary end. So
if i am with you
only this while,
or until our hair goes white,
our mothers have died,
children grown,
their children been born,
or when you spy someone
who is me
but with fresh eyes that see
you as Coatlicue once did—
and my heart
shrivels with vanity;
or a man takes me out to dance
and i leave you at the table
ice melting in your glass;
or all the jasmine in the world
has lost its scent,
let us place this born of us
at Ixtacihuatl's grave:
a footnote in the book of myths
sum of our existence—
"Even the greatest truths
contain the tremor of a lie."

* The legend of the twin volcanoes, Popocatepetl and Ixtacihuatl in
Puebla, Mexico, has it that these were once a warrior and princess of
rivaling tribes who came to a similar end as the two lovers of
Shakespeare's *Romeo and Juliet*.

LA CARTA

Vea, Ud. He regresado
una vez más
a su hogar,
a que conoció
de niña, corriendo
por las calles mojadas
brincando charcos
ignorando los gritos
de su abuela
y escapando la correa
del abuelo.

Su basílica, Mamá
se está hundiendo,
fue inevitable
las muchachas usan
el pelo corto y fuman
en la calle . . .
los hombres
siguen igual.

Todo está muy
moderno
coches por donde quiera
el metro, edificios lujosos
restaurantes elegantes.

Creo, si regresara
la daría mucho orgullo
de ver el desarrollo,
el retorno de una
gloria antigua.
Pero creo, que igualmente
sentiría tristeza, Mamá,
nada ha cambiado.

TRAFICANTE, TOO

A Sandra que escribió Traficante I

1971

Dieciocho
casi casi
señorita, pero
padece un dolor
donde no se dice.

El doctor con
dedo de fierro
lo busca.
Anuncia
con gestos gitanos
'' ¡No tendrá hijos
nunca! Y si acaso,
será peligroso.
Siguiendo con este
tema, señorita, ¿no
sabe usted que un
hombre no quiere lo
que ya está usa'o?''

En casa esperaban
madre y hermana.
''Fue solo empacho''
les contó ella
encerrandose en el
uatoclos,* donde la
pícara navaja jugó
con los muñecas
hasta la hora
de cenar.

* from " water closet "—Mexican slang

WYOMING CROSSING THOUGHTS

i will never
in my life
marry
a Mexican man,
utter
with deep devotion
"Si, mi señor."

i will never
look into his
fervent gaze
compared to the
sunrise.
i can say this,
daughter of one,
sister of another,
mother of a son.
i can say this
and not care.

i will never hold
a Mexican lover
in my arms
tell him
i love him
and mean it.

i won't serve him
a plate of beans
stand by warming
the tortillas
on the comal.

Not i.
Not i.

i will desire him
my own way
give him
what i please
meet him when
and where
no one else sees,

drive an obsidian blade
through his heart,
lick up the blood.

A MARRIAGE OF MUTES

In the house
that was his house
where the woman who lived there
cut the vegetables
hacked the chicken
boiled on the stove
and waited across the table
as he ate, with eyes that asked,
Was it all right? Was it enough?—
the woman who slept with him
changed the linen
scrubbed oil from his coveralls
hung laundry on the line
never sought the face of the woman
across the yard who hung sheets,
coveralls and underwear—
in the house where this man lived
so at peace with himself
the air grew sparse one morning.

The hall to the bathroom narrowed
as his feet grew angular and
head lightened.
He startled himself to hear his first
" caw! "—beating black wings against walls,
knocking down picture frames of the woman's
ancestors, the offspring's bronzed shoes
off the buffet.
One could only guess what he might
have said had his beak contained teeth.
The woman who always anticipated
his needs opened a window.

She would have wanted the crow to sit
on the couch
to read with her,
listen to music,
languish in a moment of peace
before the bird who was the man
she had lived with in such gratitude flew off,
but, of course, it was too much to ask.

It had always been too much to ask.

MARTES EN TOLEDO

Amanecí
sola en Toledo.
Sol contra pared
contra piedra, rechaza todo.

Un viejo nos dijo—maricas—
mientras que tomabamos un cafe
esperando el autobus de las 17.00.
¿Sera que no llevabamos los labios
pintados, que las mejillas fuesen
roidas por el viento? Ser
americana, ¿acaso, te ofendió?

Yo
te había perdonado todo.
Pero esto de llegar a tu vejez y no ser
nada, no Dali, con pesetas y castillos
admiradores alrededor del mundo
pero molinero, gerente del Banco de
Bilbao
o camarero en Madrid—

Sin dientes llegaste a los 60.
Y un juego de ajedrez con Manolo no
alivia esa herida que ha sido
tu vida: lo crudo, lo sangriente,
la guerra, el fallo, la mujer bella
a quien amaste tanto y quien se hizo
vieja
para despreciarte. Me llamaste marica.
Todo tu odio envuelto en una palabra
lanzado desde tu rincón en el cafe.

Se me cae la cuchara y al levantarla,
siento, tu muerte.

TEJIDO DE PELO Y DIENTES

Esperandote a tí
me corté
la trenza
con el mismo cuchillo
con que parto
la lengua se hierbe
hora tras hora
que apesta los cuartos
y que no como
pero le gusta al hombre
con cebollitas en sus tacos.

Esperándote a tí
me quite las faldas y los fondos
con sus encajes y falsas
transparencias.

Por tí
dejo camas desconocidas
para recostarme sobre
la vega de tu cuerpo.
—Y ni siquiera tenemos cama—
me has dicho. Contigo no
he llegado a jugar
a las muñecas
vestidas en las crinolinas de Mamá.

Llego madura. Llego limpia
sencilla sin lo sucio de lo perverso.
Llego sin mitos y misterios.
¿No me lo crees? ¡No me lo crees!
Verás, mi negra dulzura,
mi agridulce blanca. Veras.

GUADALUPE

Para Lupe Garnica

Me faltarías, Guadalupe
Vela que nunca se apaga
Risa de la madrugada
Color de la cosecha
poderosa y llena.
Me faltarías, Guadalupe . . .
tanto esperar
para que llegaras
a dejarme tu alma
envuelto en un costal.

"Mamá" no te digo.
Vale que no eres santa.
Andas por Nueva York
con tu rebaño de gatos,
perros, y niños abandonados.

Tu amor por el cigarro y el vino.
¡Ay! Guadalupe, me faltarías como un destino.

Ya te siento tan lejos
como aqui conmigo.
Te siento por el otro lado
de la luna
Entre mes venas, atrás de
mis pupilas, profundamente
en mis oídos,
donde cuando camino y llamen
tu nombre,
yo, respondaré.

CHERRY STAINED LIPS AND THICK THIGHS

That woman with perfect mouth
stained as if with cherry juice
whom you spied slipping off
red kimono, thick thighs
stepping into afternoon bath
of gardenia essence—
that woman who bore
a child the color Navajo,
went out on Saturday nights,
left you with your books and cigarettes
for Arabian men with money,
a black man who gave her jazz,
and finally settled for the white one
who loved her best
with her thick thighs and fallen breasts
she never let you see
thinking they hung ugly from early
childbearing
"not flawless
like yours," she said,
while you soaked
in your evening bath
with book in hand,
as *she* painted, brushed, sprayed herself
for men whom she demanded at 2 a.m.
they make love to her this way and that.
On the other side of the wall she whispered,
"*Down there, I want your tongue down there.*"

Yet you saw her eyes when
you entered a room, how she caught
her breath. That woman gave you
to her brother one drunken night,
who took you to a hotel.
And as he plunged, your
muted mouth
called her name.

LUNES

mujer cada
díanoche
te acercas
vienes
espero
sabes o no
sabes
tendras miedo
sere yo
eclipse

la tasa de café
frío
entierro la cabeza
entre los brazos

apenas el lunes

¿DÓNDE EMPEZAR?

Tantas lágrimas, tantas
que llora
y ¿dónde empiezo a acumularlas?
En tinas y cubetas
en ollas de peltre y jarras de barro
se acaban las toallas y las esponjas
el periódico del domingo y mis revistas de moda.

Al fin, mis senos empapados, mi cabello,
mis hombros, las manos que recorren su rostro,
mi boca se abre a tomar su llanto salado.
Tantas lágrimas y en cada gota un cuento
de fracaso.

La casa se hundía y nos busqué
una almadía.
Nos fuimos a la deriva adormecidas por la madrugada.
Nos fuimos a la deriva sobre angustias y sueños pesados.
Yo cantándole en murmullos: —Ya no llores, mujer.
Ya no estés triste. Porque vas a acabarte llorando.
Ya no llores, ya, ya, ya . . .

I AM THE DAUGHTER/MOTHER WHO HAS LEARNED

i am the daughter/mother
who has learned
devotion,
tenderness,
to mend
the irreparable
and to cultivate.

i know how to labor
with clenched teeth,
to find strength
and gratitude in relief.

But i don't know how
to love.

Does this paper with
printed words without lyric or sound
love?

Does my daughter/mother/lover
believe it so
because i've learned
the things i know?

i've learned from conch shells,
prisms, coral,
and granite;
the night without stars,
black pupils of eyes,
dirt embedded in the hard soles
of *guarached* feet.
Politicians, shamans,
and poets call these
mysteries.

The daughter/mother who falls
into bed does not recall love
with practiced gestures
and memorized utterings.

i am the daughter/mother who
cuts the umbilical cord
of umbilical cords
to set us both free.

Released to nowhere,
we can return
to each other
baptized with new names
like nuns sanctified
by virtue of
having named ourselves.

Accusations
of knowing or not,
lessons as
daughters/mothers/lovers
will cease.
If there be
no love even then,
at least
we shall have peace.

IV
In My Country

A CHRISTMAS GIFT
FOR THE PRESIDENT OF THE UNITED STATES,
CHICANO POETS, AND A MARXIST OR TWO
I'VE KNOWN IN MY TIME

i've left philosophy to men,
heirs to their classics,
lovers of silk-laden
self-aggrandizing perceptions.
Poetry, too, belongs to them,
which is attributed
to their feminine side,
mystification of nature, and
relentless desire to be divine.

Their poems that come at night
from a memory of a
suckled breast
ring of epitaphs;
verses pretending to speak
to a friend have no other end
than to be recognized.

So these are not poems, i readily admit,
as i grapple with non-existence,
making scratches with stolen pen.
One word is a splinter of steel
that flings from the drill press
into my father's eye;
that one, embedded in the thumb
of my child's father.
Another word, also steel,
the rolling pin
my grandmother used for the
last tortillas of her life.
Exclamation points—my
departure from the Church at 18!

Simple expressions, these.

Rape is not a poem.
Incest does not rhyme.
Nor the iridescent blue labor
of the placenta that follows
giving birth. These are not thoughts
great books have withstood time for,
so unlike the embellishment of war
or man's melancholy at being
neither earth nor heaven bound.

My verses have no legitimacy.
A white woman inherits
her father's library,
her brother's friends. Privilege
gives language that escapes me.
Past my Nahua eyes
and Spanish surname, English syntax
makes its way to my mouth
with the grace of a clubbed foot.

So it doesn't matter now
how many lines i read,
institutions i attend.
Something inherent resists
the insistence that i don't exist.

i shall read for pleasure,
write for pleasure,
spend countless hours contemplating
shadows changing the room
with the movement of the sun.
i shall make love
and never tell of it.
My legacies are anonymous.
Nothing matters
while one man can yet
lie to the world,
and the world
chooses to believe him.

EVERYWHERE I GO

Preguntan de donde soy,
y no se que responder.
De tanto no tener nada,
no tengo de a donde ser.

—Atahualpa Yupanqui

My new speech is echoed
with the tongue that sounds
of tumbling wooden blocks,
a peculiar conjugation
of consonantls running tlogether.

Everywhere i go
i am asked my origin
as if i bore antennae
or the eye
of the Cyclops.

Somewhere i squat
to plant seeds, dry
animals skins, paint
clay pots with floral dashes
of red and aquamarine,
place a firm hand—
with an incantation
life emerges.

i walk with gold adornments
pierced through my nose,
gems embedded in drilled holes
in my teeth.

i am loved.

And i love, and am not lost,
nor wander.

EL SUEÑO

Lucía
mi traje zapoteco
un huipil
rojo
rojo
color de sangre
zapoteca
brillante
alumbrante
del sol
oaxaqueño
más suave
que los pétalos
de la flor
macizo
como los nopales viejos
que adornan
la sierra
dulce
como el maguey
caliente como el
mezcal.

Lucía mi huipil colorado
por las calles
de una ciudad
tan orgullosa
tan fuerte
que no sentí
el primer golpe
del rechazo.

ENTRE PRIMAVERA Y OTOÑO

La india carga
su bandara sobre
su cara
manchada de sangre
sus cicatrices corren
como las carreteras viejas
de su tierra
y la india no se queja.

Le preguntan por qué
no cuenta
su historia
y ojos húmedos responden
que le cuentan todo
al que quiere oir.

Si acaso abre
su boca
sale la canción
del mar
los ecos del viento
hay volcanes inquietos
en el pecho de la india.

Sus huesos se han
hecho del polvo
de cincuenta mil muertos
el grito doloroso
de ellos
es el silencio
de la india.

Ayer tuvo un hombre
que le hizo sueños
del aire . . .
tuvo sus hombres
la india
pero ahora no tiene
a nadie.

Del mundo es la india
y si la ves
bailando
en vestido de seda
o pidiendo en la calle
no le preguntes el porque
o tal razón por su camino.

El destino de la india
es la bandera que carga
sobre su cara quemada
dura de sangre seca
y la india no se queja
no se queja de nada.

ZOILA LÓPEZ

If i were you, Zoila,
i wouldn't be here
in English class
with the disturbed child
who sits in the back
with the husband
who doesn't work.
i wouldn't laugh, Zoila,
if my first winter up north
were without boots
and the only thing to
warm me was the photograph
of Jorgito dressed as a
little indian in white
pajamas and sandals on
Guadalupe's Day, just before
he was killed by a truck
that carried oranges.

i wouldn't bathe, change
my dress, look for work,
hold a pencil upright
after this summer when
the baby ran a high fever
and the hospital people in
that marbles-in-the-mouth
language said, "It's okay.
Take her home."
She died that night.
You'd thought she'd just
stopped crying.

i would die, if i were you,
Zoila, a million deaths at
the end of each nightmarish day
with its miniscule hopes like
snowflakes that melt on one's
teeth and tongue and taste of
nothing.

ME & BABY

Chicago, 1983

It's me, the pregnant Puerto Rican girls,
short Mexicans with braids down to there,
and all the babies in the world
waiting for our numbers to be called.

At 3 p.m. i get a chair past
Egberto with bad breath
from beer the night before,
Marta and her sister with
strollers between them, the
autistic boy of the twisted cheeks.
Women divided from us by desks
type out coupons for cereal, milk, juice,
government approved and labeled
at the market.

The chewing gum popper i'll pop
if my name's not called soon,
mispronounced as it is each month.
The clerks are bilingual but
high school diplomas left them
illiterate.

A woman in the back complains
about her man's habits, another
wishes she had welfare. The Salvadorans
don't say a word, just wait out their turn.
The Guatemalan in the corner feeds
her infant Coke and chips. A balanced diet
poster above her head.

The nutritionist on hand does not speak
Quechua and who can blame her? There's
only so much one can do.

4:45: The husband who came to leave
the kids with his wife, never lifted
his eyes. We must be an ugly sight.
His green pants and paper lined shoes

soaked through with December slush.

It's dark now. Rush hour crawls past
the windows. Baby needs solids
the doctor at the clinic has said.
i'll speak up when i get my chance.
i'll pound my fist on their coupon
covered desks if they talk to me of
forms, and doctor's written requests,
and more forms, and appointments.

i kick the wall at 5 of 5 instead.
The office is officially closed. The
coupon books are put away.
The clerks freshen their lipstick.
The nutritionist locks her cubicle.

We, who are left,
must come back,
take a new number,
get away from the entrance. If
there are no empty chairs,
please don't block the way. Sorry, Ma'am.
We open at 8.
We'll see you tomorrow.
Best to arrive *temprano*.

PACO AND ROSA

"AS SOON AS THE CHILDREN
ARE OUT OF SCHOOL
I'LL COME," Rosa shouts
over static
from La Barca to Chicago.
"GOOD," says her husband,
hangs up, sighs.

Tonight he won't
shave, slap on Christmas
cologne, press down his hair.
He won't go to the Paraiso Club
with his brother or to the
corner tavern where a man gets
lost in the smell of hairspray
on a woman whose name he'd
rather not know.

Instead, hands behind his head,
he thinks of Rosa
who smells of the children
the meat-packing plant where
she worked between babies,
the summer they met, La Barca
by the sea. Rosa,
who smells of home.

COLD

Cold
is not once
or twice in a life
not from a window
of a fleeting train
glimmer of sun
so white blinding on
an afternoon it must be
heaven, not
a picture postcard with rose
cheeked children on sleds
or a sleigh ride to a distant
house with smoking chimney, not
a crystal paperweight turned
upside down a flurry falls on
a row of little houses and
evergreens.

It is cold
in the city surrounded by
flatland, nothing but silos
to stave off the wind. Mucus
drips from a child's nose
during its rasping sleep.
Rats curl and nest behind
the stove.
Feet lose feeling for weeks.
Joints stiffen, backs create
new places to ache. A constant
quiver inhabits the body.

Windows rattle and call out
demons. The cracked-on back
covered with cardboard and tape.

Cold
is not nostalgic.

Winter emits no fond memories.
Although you will laugh
only to find teeth ring
sharply with pain.

TOMÁS DE UTRERA'S FIRST POEM OF SPRING

Death comes to us every day
in banal greyness. A boy
jumps into the street
a car runs the light . . .
death comes to us. Siren
aflame and bright. I go
on my way.

A familiar bar,
a shot is 50 cents.
I teach English to Haitians
and other immigrants.
The boy on the tar
a repulsive mass like the boil
on my wife's back so bad
she hasn't been to work in 3 days.
Death comes to us in tricky ways.

In Spain, a day was just a day
but the nights! Oh, the nights!
There was Manos de Plata, not even
a Spaniard, makes more money
than any gypsy on the guitar.
(That boy on the tar,
a black lump, foot quivers, stops.)

Arturo with pointed beard,
cognac in hand, laughs
to see me. I also laugh.
Death comes . . .
I owe him 3 bucks or maybe
he owes me.
Anyway, the gypsies on Southport
are not like the gypsies of Spain
        always thinking of money
        eyes on your pockets.
Turn me upside down, bastards
of a saintly mother, turn

me upside down
Amerika! América,
        ¿no sabes que mañana no me da miedo?

So he tells the bartender
to make it 2 and put
it on the tab.
Violin under his arm
like a bundle of rags.
I'll be drunk before I'm
home, and won't have told
about the boy.

Arturo's son works in
computers. He's proud.
(Not Arturo, his son, I mean.)
Lives in a highrise
with a doorman named Racine.
Racine smiles all the time
with heavy lidded eyes.

        I have two daughters.
One dances flamenco / disco
the other bangs on the piano.
We watch Wonder Woman at 4:00.
The P.T.A. wanted a vote on a
mimeograph machine. I wanted
an uprising of the Guatemalans.
My name is . . .
        (Death comes to us in our sleep
        clenched between our teeth
        caught in the gold fillings)

I never had a son. What
would I tell him anyway? I have
a daughter, *Angela de la Gloria*—
Dance, Angela, baila! Mamá will gather
the silver coins while Papá
beats on the guitar.

I teach English now and
            death comes . . .
but so what?

SO WHAT AMERIKA?
I am a plague! Vermin!
Live on forever!
You can't make me die.

The following morning
in the newspaper, not a scribble.
The Haitians saw nothing.
That corner . . . not so much
as a bloodstain, a witness,
because I didn't see it, not I.
You can't fool me, Death,
you can't fool me. Come, let's
celebrate! Today is your birthday.

WE WOULD LIKE YOU TO KNOW

We would like you to know
we are not all
docile
nor revolutionaries
but we are all survivors.
We do not all carry
zip guns, hot pistols,
steal cars.
We do know how
to defend ourselves.

We do not all have
slicked-back hair
distasteful apparel
unpolished shoes
although the economy
doesn't allow everyone
a Macy's chargecard.

We do not all pick
lettuce, run
assembly lines, clean
restaurant tables, even
if someone has to do it.

We do not all sneak
under barbed wire or
wade the Rio Grande.

These are the facts.

We would like you to know
we are not all brown.
Genetic history has made
some of us blue eyed as any
German immigrant
and as black as a descendant
of an African slave.
We never claimed to be
a homogeneous race.

We are not all victims,
all loyal to one cause,
all perfect; it is a
psychological dilemma
no one has resolved.

We would like to give
a thousand excuses
as to why we all find
ourselves in a predicament
residents of a controversial
power
how we were all caught
with our pants down
and how petroleum was going
to change all that but
you've heard it all before and
with a wink and a snicker
left us babbling amongst
ourselves.

We would like you to know
guilt or apologetic gestures
won't revive the dead
redistribute the land
or natural resources.
We are left
with one final resolution
in our own predestined way,
we are going forward.
There is no going back.

NO SOLO EL SER CHILENA

Pablo le escribe a la mosca como le
escribe al imperialismo

—Victoria Miranda

i leave home
because home is not a four-walled structure
or the place where those who call themselves
friends welcome me.
i leave home because where i am not safe,
is where i am most safe
safety being inconsequential, finally,
a sea being the same sea throughout the planet
fertile ground lasting as sweet on any continent
the doe eyes of any child being the same
that form in my belly now.
i would apologize for being
less god than animal but naturally
this is not my way.
Sometimes, i recall, as if in a dream
face wet, body trembling, how once
raw meat satisfied my appetite.

SOMEONE TOLD ME

Gracias a la vida que me ha dado tanto
me dió dos luceros que cuando los abro
perfecto distingo, lo negro del blanco
                                                    —V.P.

Someone told me the other night,
over flor de caña rum and listening
to her records, that Violeta Parra
killed herself.
She put a gun to her head
at midnight.
All the neighbors came running
at the sound of the report.
It had something to do with economics
and the desertion of her young lover
for a woman half her age. There was
talk of jealous scenes.
Violeta Parra who composed " Gracias
a la vida" killed herself.
Liberals and politicos might be
disappointed in this account. That
she did not die beneath the blows
of rifle butts or by electric shock,
and instead, died the death
of a woman.

ESTA MANO

¿poemas?
no tengo
poemas
tengo
esta mano que
escribe
a veces
recuerda
acariciar entre
sombras
cada dedo en busca
cada una cazadora
mano traicionera—
¡Pinta! ¡Cuenta! ¡Di algo!
Me ahogas en tu silencio
acercate, mano necia
sí, así, suave sobre mi
rostro, recorre las piernas
también recuerdan
no como tú, tan segura
orgullosa—tiemblan
no les apena rogar, entre
garse humildemente cada
vez más— ¿Sabes un secreto?
Ven, con confianza oye—
creo que eres romántica yo
olvido o será que me voy
lejos lejos la ausencia me
libre o si no este verso sería
de ella— *la otra*
de dedos, piernas, suspiros pesados
y lo demás mierda ¡Qué va! Su cuerpo
un ojo entero vigilando momento tras
momento monumento. Su cuerpo que es
su petate, piso, caja, cárcel, casa,
canasta, campo, columpio, costal, co

mal, tamal, topacio, tan tin tan
to que aguantar tendrá que brotar
poemas, llorar poemas, vomitar y orinar poemas
¿poemas?
no tengo
poemas
tengo
esta mano
recuerda

IN MY COUNTRY

This is not my country.
In my country, men
do not play at leaders
women do not play at men
there is no god
crucified to explain
the persistence of cruelty.

In my country
i don't hesitate to sit
alone in the park, to go
to the corner store at night
for my child's milk, to wear
anything that shows my breasts.

In my country
i do not stand for cutbacks,
layoffs, and pay union dues
companies do not close down
to open up again in far-off
places where eating is the
main objective.

In my country
men do not sleep with guns
beneath their pillows. They
do not accept jobs building weapons.
They don't lose their mortgages, pensions,
their faith or their dignity.

In my country
children are not abused
beaten into adulthood
left with sitters who resent them
for the meager salary a single parent
can afford. They do not grow up
to repeat the pattern.

In my country
i did not wait in line for milk
coupons for my baby, get the wrong
prescription at the clinic, was not
forced to give my ethnic origin,
nor died an unnatural death.

In my country, i am not exotic.
i do not have Asian eyes. i
was not raised on a reservation.
i do not go artificially blonde.
The sun that gravitates to my dark
pigmentation is not my enemy.

i do not watch television, entertain
myself at commercial movie houses,
invest in visual art or purchase
literature at grocery stores.

In my country, i do not stand
for the cold because i can't
afford the latest gas hike. i
am not expected to pay taxers
three times over.

This is not my world.
In my world, Mesoamerica
was a magnificent Quetzal,
Africa and its inhabitants
were left alone. Arab women
don't cover their faces or
allow their sexual parts to be
torn out. In my world,
no one is prey.

Death is not a relief.
i don't bet on reincarnation
or heaven, or lose the present
in apathy or oblivion.

i do not escape into my sleep.
Analysts are not made rich by
my discoveries therein. My
mother is not cursed for giving
birth. i am not made ashamed
for being.

In my world, i do not attend
conferences with academicians
who anthropologize my existence
dissect the simplicity of greed
and find the differences created
out of Babel interesting.

In my world
i am a poet
who can rejoice in the coming of
Halley's comet, the wonders
of Machu Picchu, and a sudden kiss.

In my world, i breathe clean air.
i don't anticipate nuclear war.
i speak all languages. i don't
negate aging, listen to myths
to explain my misery or create them.

In my world the poet sang loud
and clear and everyone heard
without recoiling. It was sweet
as harvest, sharp as tin, strong
as the northern wind, and all had
a coat warm enough to bear it.